D0759550

It's Not Personal, Sonny.
It's Business

It's Not Personal, Sonny.
It's Business

HOW TO RUN YOUR FAMILY, LIFE AND BUSINESS LIKE A SICILIAN

STEPH PALERMO

Columbus, Ohio

It's Not Personal, Sonny. It's Business © Copyright 2020 Stephanie Palermo

All rights reserved. No part of this publication may be reproduced, distributed or transmitted in any form or by any means, including photocopying, recording, or other electronic or mechanical methods, without the prior written permission of the publisher, except in the case of brief quotations embodied in critical reviews and certain other noncommercial uses permitted by copyright law.

Although the author and publisher have made every effort to ensure that the information in this book was correct at press time, the author and publisher do not assume and hereby disclaim any liability to any party for any loss, damage, or disruption caused by errors or omissions, whether such errors or omissions result from negligence, accident, or any other cause.

Adherence to all applicable laws and regulations, including international, federal, state and local governing professional licensing, business practices, advertising, and all other aspects of doing business in the US, Canada or any other jurisdiction is the sole responsibility of the reader and consumer.

Neither the author nor the publisher assumes any responsibility or liability whatsoever on behalf of the consumer or reader of this material. Any perceived slight of any individual or organization is purely unintentional.

The resources in this book are provided for informational purposes only and should not be used to replace the specialized training and professional judgment of a health care or mental health care professional.

Neither the author nor the publisher can be held responsible for the use of the information provided within this book. Please always consult a trained professional before making any decision regarding treatment of yourself or others.

For more information, email steph@juststeph.com.

The cover design and editorial work for this book are entirely the product of the author. Gatekeeper Press did not participate in and is not responsible for any aspect of these elements.

ISBN (hardcover): 9781662900723
ISBN (paperback): 9781662900730
eISBN: 9781662900747

Library of Congress Control Number: 2020907048

Also by Steph Palermo:

The Only Way is Up: Just Steph's Perspective on Life

Coming Soon:

Where The Hell Are Those Ruby Slippers:?
The Search for the Power

Dedication

The only appropriate person in my life to dedicate this book to is my grandmother, Mary Toscano Palermo. She was born to Francesco and Francesca Toscano in Riesi, Sicily. They settled in Boston's North End where most Italian immigrants pitched their figurative tents.

Grandma was a dominant person in our family. She was strong willed and pushy. Grandma loved drama. She screamed at wakes, cried at the drop of a dime. After Grandpa passed, she wanted everyone to think her life was so bad. Her favorite saying was, "I pray every day God will take me." Inevitably, I would be rolling my eyes behind her thinking, "does she know where she's going?" Poor Grandma!

While Grandma had that less-than-admirable side, she could be so sweet, and she loved her family. Grandma loved my sister and me to death. She would scream when she saw me, "Steph, you are a movie star!" She called my sister Miss America. Grandma, as dysfunctional as she was, truly wanted to be in our lives. We were her life.

Grandma worked tirelessly to continue all the Sicilian traditions taught to her. She was the best baker. Who can bake without a recipe? Grandma. She baked all the rustic Sicilian sweets like *cassateddi con ricotta, ricotta pie and sfingi.* Lamb at Easter, seafood on Christmas Eve, and *zeppoli di San Giuseppe* on March 19, St Joseph's Day.

Grandma was connected to Sicily and talked relentlessly about Riesi. The old country was the foundation for everything Grandma did and taught. We were involved, as a family, with The St. Joseph Society of Boston of which Papa Cicino (my great-grandfather, Mary's father) was one of the founders. Riesi, the cousins, traditions, and the food were all drilled into my head. They became part of me.

Grandma is the reason why I was so attracted to Sicily. Her love for all that is steeped in Sicilian life became my drive to spend extended time in Sicily, learn more about the life and remember what I forgot she taught me. Grandma is the reason you all are getting these lessons in this book.

Thank you, Grandma. I love and miss you. I want so badly to ask you questions. I long tell you how much I appreciate what you gave to me. I would love to share with you how much I love Sicily and the lessons I learned growing up Sicilian. But, I guess you already know.

Table of Contents

Foreword

When Steph told me about her new book, while in the planning stages, I asked what I could do to support her. I was floored when she asked if I could write a foreword. Steph and I not only share our Italian heritage, we are both of Sicilian descent. We grew up in the same neighborhood, outside Boston, that was mainly comprised of Italians, many of which were immigrants from Sicily. We were cut from the same cloth, so to speak, and enjoyed similar traditions from the old country. As we both got older and reconnected, we found there were many more things we shared besides just love of our neighborhood, family and our Sicilian roots and traditions. One was trying to make the people around us better. No matter if it is by simple kindness, or developing a professional curriculum designed for you to live your best life, the goal is the same: to make us all better husbands, wives, father, sons, mothers and daughters.

While reading *It's Not Personal, Sonny. It's Business*, my biggest challenge was not calling Steph all hours of night to discuss my every thought on how she nailed it! Today, we do not communicate the way we should. Our written communication has been reduced to Twitter-type dialogue, poor grammar, and terse responses. There is still importance to looking a person in the eye and communicating clearly, and with honesty.

In business, I deal with anyone from Chief Executives to System Analysts, and the one thing that is expected is honesty and integrity from both sides. Maybe it is because the importance of having meals together was instilled in me throughout my childhood. Many, many a relationship has been built sitting around the table and breaking bread. We come to understand business issues and how they can be solved, as well as learning who we are as people. This helps gain a trust between all parties, and how we can do the right thing by one another. My goal is to support our business partners in a way that helps them grow their careers. They know that, and they trust I have their best interests at heart.

Also, as a team, there is nothing more important than breaking bread with the work family. No matter if you work in an office, or from home, you want to know that you are part of something bigger, and not just left on an island. As a remote worker, I cherish the time I get to spend with my extended work family, around a table, laughing and telling stories about everything from our childhoods, to home life, to crazy events that happened in our careers. This has made us a much closer unit, with virtually no employee turnover in the past five years. When you feel like you are part of something more than a paycheck, the pull on you to move on and jump from job to job is mitigated. Bringing in new employees is very costly, from recruiting, to hiring, to time lost in the position not being filled, not to mention the cost of training and development. Making a person feel like they are part of the family pays off in the long run.

I applaud Steph in her efforts to teach others how to incorporate our Sicilian ways and traditions into our personal and work lives, and I hope the reader takes what she says to heart. And for God's sake, hire someone like Steph to teach you how make your dinner table, or table in the boardroom a place to communicate and thrive!

Chris Ridgway
Senior Sales Engineer
Wakefield, MA

Introduction

Papa *Cicino* (a Sicilian nickname for Francesco) immigrated to the United States with his family in 1920, when Grandma was a baby.

Both sides of my family immigrated to America from Sicily. Like most Italian and Sicilian pioneers, they wanted to be Americans. Sicilians from the old country were proud to be in America, the land of opportunity. For most, leaving home was their last resort to find work and provide for their hungry families.

Boston's North End is one-third of a square mile. Each small town in Sicily claims its unique traditions most of which revolve around the town's patron saint. When Italians and Sicilians alike finally made it to Boston, they settled near their families and *paesani* (friends from the same village).

If the North End is one-third of a square mile, what does that mean? They literally lived in the same buildings, adjacent to folks from their *paesi* (home towns). Aunts, uncles, cousins,

friends all lived within a holler of each other. And that they did: holler. There were no phones; they merely opened the window and yelled to each other.

They adopted American traditions and melded them with their own. One example is Sunday sauce. In Sicily *sugo Domenica* was served at 1:30 with fresh pasta, sometimes with meatballs and sausages in the sauce. Meanwhile, Americans were eating roasts with gravy. To help their children fit in with their new neighbors, many Italo-Americans began to call Sunday sauce gravy. Unfortunately, many immigrants did not speak their native language to their children fearing they would not fully immerse in the American way of life.

Growing up steeped in Sicilian traditions shaped my life and journey more than my birth difference, education and economic status (or lack thereof) combined. Events like Christmas Eve, taking my great grandmother *zeppole* (fried dough balls) on St. Joseph Day and the screaming crying at wakes and funerals paved my perceptions, thought processes and judgments on every aspect of life. Most Americans lived paycheck to paycheck. We lived meal to meal, discussing what we were going to eat at the next meal while enjoying the food in front of us. This has not changed, by the way.

I was totally shocked when I went to college. I learned that there were moms out there that did not know how to cook. It was amazing to hear stories of lousy dinners, moms who worked outside the house and jarred tomato sauce. Gross!

I found out quickly that people could stab you in the back and get away with it. Because they were raised not having to be present at the dinner table, getting a smack in the head when you talked back to your mother or the pointed finger for making disgruntled faces, respect for authority was unheard of. We were always ready to kick someone's ass if said person messed with our siblings, cousins or best friends, loyalty in action.

Before I continue, you need to know that Marlon Brando as Don Corleone, Frank Sinatra, Dean Martin, etc. are icons for Italian-Americans. Carlo, Connie's husband in The Godfather, deserved to get whacked (killed), Henry Hill was a rat, and Sophia Loren is a timeless goddess. We love Giada DiLaurentis, Andrea Bocelli and Pavarotti.

When Americans think of Sicilian immigrants, their education comes from Hollywood where the Mafia is idolized. With all peoples there are definitely negative traits. The Mafia movies afford a glimpse of many of the dark aspects of Sicilian life. However, this is such a tiny portion of immigrants. Most came here to work legitimately: brick layers, carpenters, fishermen, bakers, restauranteurs. Italian and Sicilian immigrants were so

proud to be Americans they felt it an honor to go to war to defend the very nation that gave them a home. My grandfather on my mother's side actually liked paying taxes. For him, this was giving back to the country that afforded him work.

In this book, I strive to bring to light the best of Sicilian life and traditions. At times I will poke fun at some of the less than proud actions taken by many of us. However, I firmly believe if we meld the old school Sicilian ways with the great advances in the modern era, lives, families, and businesses will change for the better.

We can move into the new decade loving life, hoping for the future and appreciating age-old traditions. You can expect better personal relationships, an increased pride in yourself, higher productivity and profits at work and a sense of belonging to something bigger than you. Come back with me to go forward.

Know I love you all!
Wishing you love, balance & peace.
Amore & Baci,
Just Steph

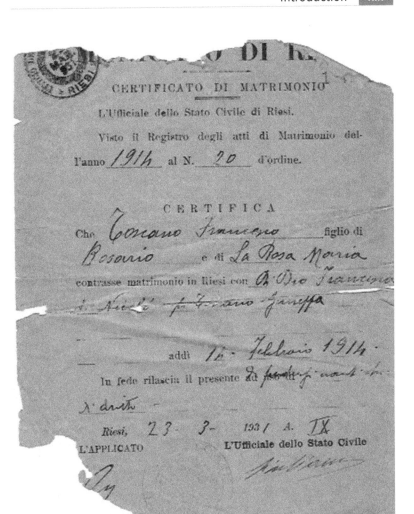

CERTIFICATO DI MATRIMONIO

L'Ufficiale dello Stato Civile di Riesi.

Visto il Registro degli atti di Matrimonio del-
l'anno *1914* al N. *20* d'ordine.

CERTIFICA

Che *Cosano Francesco* figlio di
Rosario e di *La Rosa Maria*
contrasse matrimonio in Riesi con *D. Dio Francesca*

addì *16 Febbraio 1914*

In fede rilascia il presente

Riesi, *23 - 3 - 193* / A. IX

L'APPLICATO   L'Ufficiale dello Stato Civile

Preface

So you do not think I am talking out of both sides of my mouth, I would like to explain my use of the mafia movie quotes in my book. The writing in these movies is genius. Sicilians, to some degree, subscribe to these beliefs. However, if you extrapolate the wisdom beneath the intimidation and violence, one can find a path to success in life. I also think these lines are funny, and when used appropriately, are on target.

I posted this question on social media that included many Italian and Sicilian pages: "What aspects of growing up Sicilian positively impacted your life?" I got so many responses. The quotes in this book, other than the mafia movies, are real quotes from real Sicilian-Americans. One last point, I explain chronologically, from the time we are born into our Sicilian skin until we eat our last dish of pasta, how the beliefs and wisdom of the old country shaped my life and will benefit yours.

It Takes A Village

"A man who doesn't spend time with his family can never be a real man."

Don Vito Corleone, Godfather I

From the moment Sicilian babies take their first breathe, "the family" is the central focus of existence. The family is the primary institution for learning. Anyone married or over 25 can be your teacher whether your mother is standing there or not. If I got out of line, and my aunt saw me, I was in just as much trouble as if my mom witnessed my actions. This was my village.

"Family and religion was the utmost importance in our life. Everything we did was family oriented. I have kept this as the Cosentino motto for my children and grandchildren."

Cindy Cosentino

We spent Sundays, holidays, vacations and snow days together. I chomped at the bit waiting for my cousins to arrive. When they did, it was instantaneous laughing, playing, singing and eating. I don't remember anyone crying or fighting. We attended each other's concerts, plays, sporting events and birthday parties. Religious milestones such as Baptisms, First Communions and Confirmations brought together not only the immediate and extended family but other families and friends. This was our sacred tribe.

> *"Being around family, I always tell my husband that growing we knew everyone or treated everyone like family. I knew all of my cousin's friends and even growing up knowing all of my cousins-in-law as well. Getting together once a week..."*
>
> Stephanie Corelli

It was during these events when I learned to communicate with my elders. I developed my sense of humor, learned right from wrong and loyalty. I learned appreciation for the previous generation's taste in music, entertainment and meatballs. My family was the most important institution in my life. It was the benchmark for how I believed other families and institutions operated. Boy, was I shocked to realize this was not true outside my Sicilian neighborhood.

Applications

Family

It is very difficult to pick up twenty or thirty years or more into your life and say, " let's start living like Sicilians." However, depending on where you are in your familial relationships, you can make subtle and maybe some not-so-subtle changes. Sicilian families eat, laugh and cry together. By adopting some or all of the following suggestions, you can expect to bond as a family and grow closer:

- Stand up to your kids. You are in charge: Have a backbone.
- Allow your kids to feel the consequences of their choices and actions.
- Stop candy-coating everything. Nobody gets invited to every party, and not everyone deserves a trophy.
- Make the home and family a safe place physically and emotionally.
- Show your family whom to trust and who is reliable.
- Talk to them about your generation.
- Stop texting in the house!
- Hire someone like me to help you take charge of your family.
- If you do not know how to cook, now is the time to learn, and I don't mean going vegan or dairy-free. I mean, learn how to prepare real food, not from packages or take-out.

Life

If your family of origin is less than supportive, find a tribe. How can you find people you can trust? This is a risk, however, and the first step is to be what you want in your life. Like attracts like. You may have to do some weeding, but be the loyal, reliable, trustworthy person you would like in your life. Here are some suggestions:

- Bring people together over food.
- Talk about more than who is sleeping with whom.
- Respectfully discuss topics that interest you with your new tribe.
- Ask for help and support.
- Stop texting and relying on technology to initiate and foster relationships!
- Talk and spend time face to face. The people who are worth having in your life will stick around. The others will walk.
- Hire someone like me to help you get your life in order.
- Be the kind of person you would like in your tribe.

In Business

If you are not doing so already, start running your business like a family. Can you not see the benefits? A family sticks together. You have to be crazy or very very bad to leave the family. A family cares about the needs and well-being of its members.

Here are some tips to morph your cold crew into a warm supportive family:

- Get to know everyone personally.
- Offer events (even during work hours) that help employees to get to know one another.

- Encourage well-being for the entire person.
- Eat together.
- Encourage celebrating each other's successes.
- Be there when times are tough: illnesses, new babies, life altering events
- Foster loyalty, appreciation and service toward and for one another.
- People want to feel needed. Help your crew to understand their importance in the organization. Let them know they are part of something big, and without them, there is a void.
- Start company traditions: Friday afternoon happy hour; Monday morning healthy breakfast where people share weekend events; Midweek lunch & learn/well-being hour.
- Hire someone like me to help you form a family with your employees and co-workers.
- Be excited to see your family every day!

Pass the Pasta

"Papa never talked business at the table."

Connie, Godfather I

Mealtime was and always is sacred. We sat down for dinner together every night. The table was our sanctuary. We discussed the day's events, plans for the next day or so and important family news like what grandma was up to or that cousin Anthony got accepted to college.

Every event revolved around a meal: weddings, wakes and funerals. When someone passed away, the bereavement dinner after the burial was as important as the cemetery arrangements. I did not realize how genius this was. As an adult, I came to understand that mealtime not only bonded us as a family, it was where we healed from grief and learned table manners, sarcasm and humor.

"I learned the importance of family and friends, the love of food and of sharing with others and most importantly, I learned the importance of having God in my life."
Rosalyn DeSimone

I woke up every Sunday to the wonderful aroma of meatballs frying. My mom was up early preparing for Sunday dinner. Sunday dinner was the pinnacle meal of the week. For Sicilians this was the day we thanked God for what we had. We celebrated birthdays on Sunday with the family, regardless of on which actual day your birthday fell. The dinner table honored the blessing of *abbondanza*, abundance.

"Leave the gun. Take the cannoli."
Peter Clemenza
(Richard S. Castellano), The Godfather

Our typical Sunday dinner was composed of pasta, meatballs, sausages in the sauce. We always had fresh bread, grated cheese, and salad. Most Sundays included a meat, veal cutlets, lemon baked chicken or a pork loin. If we were lucky, Mom made stuffed artichokes, stuffed peppers, or eggplant parmigiana. For dessert, we enjoyed cannoli, grandma's homemade pies or cookies.

We ate shortly after 1:00 pm. My grandparents, uncles, aunts and cousins would trickle in. As my sister and I got older, our friends came by. After 5:00 pm, the food came back out.

I always felt a little sad when Sunday was over. I was safe with my family. I could breathe, laugh and let my hair down. Monday promised the unknown and unwanted anxiety; it was the jungle. The experiences at the dinner table were fun, consistent and reliable, something lacking today.

Applications

Family

It amazes me that families do not sit down and eat together. Sharing a meal bonds family members to each other and their guests. Use mealtime to connect, discuss and laugh. It is at the table where you will find out the dirt on everybody else. This keeps parents in the loop. Here are some guidelines for family dinners:

- Sit down as a family, at the least, a few times per week.
- Make one of those meals celebratory, a thanksgiving for all you have.

- Do not use the table as a place to discipline your kids, unless they misbehave at the table. Only correct table manners and disrespect at mealtime. If the table is a fun, safe place, everyone will want to be there.
- Invite other family members and friends. This teaches appropriate conversation, humor, and crosses generation barriers.
- If you have older folks in your world, invite them. Kids need to interact with multi generations. They tell great stories.
- Get the kids involved in the cooking and setting the table. Let them light the candles, chop and mix with your help. This make the kids want to be there, promise.
- Include your children in the conversations.
- No phones at the table.
- Hire someone like me to whip your family into shape.
- If you do not know how to cook, now is the time to learn.

Life

Busy-ness is not only an epidemic; it is a cop-out. It is an escape from sharing who you are. This is a fear-based, victim mentality. It is weak. When you slow down and interact with actual human beings, you satisfy the built in need to exist in community.

Humans are wired this way. Solitary lifestyles are contrary to human nature. This is why you are lonely, not because you cannot get a date. Mealtime is, in my opinion, the best place to build your communal relationships. You cannot develop deep meaningful relationships when you are ships passing in the night.

This isn't The Jetsons where you pop a pill for your dinner. Make the time! Here are a few ways to bring your peeps to the table:

- Look at your calendar and carve out times to share meals with friends and/or family.
- Pick up the phone and talk to your tribe about having dinner together.
- Invite friends to your home for dinner.
- Start a supper club.
- Ask friends to co-host with you to lighten the burden.
- Offer to help host at your friends' home. Offer to bring wine, an appetizer or dessert.
- Invite a few to come early to help you prepare dinner. Drink wine and talk while you cook.
- Do not allow phones at the table!
- Hire someone like me to teach you how to enrich your life at the table.

In Business

There is no better place to bond with your work family than over a meal. Food is necessary for survival, a source of nourishment and well-being, and it feeds the soul. A company that eats together regularly is a family. Employees and co-workers, subconsciously, will feel cared for because basic human needs are filled at the table.

You may be thinking there is no budget for paying for meals. Start small: lunches, enlisting work family members to help cook or cooking yourself. As your family bonds, productivity will rise; I promise! Then you can start budgeting for meals with your family.

Here's how you can deepen the bonds of your work family via the company dinner table:

- Start a weekly company meal that is scheduled midweek during business hours. Tell your family the rules: no talking business and no telephones or laptops at the table. Encourage conversations. Pick a light topic and start the discussion. Ask people how things are going at home, what are their passions and if they have hobbies.
- As your family bonds, offer an after-hours dinner, either off or on site once a quarter. Same rules apply.
- At least twice a year, host events for your work family and include their immediate families like a summer picnic and a holiday party.
- The best thing a business owner can do is host dinners at their home. This is where you really will win people over. They will feel included in your life, accepted and special. It is here where you will gel as a true family.
- Hire someone like me to show you how to begin incorporating meals with your work family.
- Be excited to see your family at the dinner table!

R.E.S.P.E.C.T

"I respect a person who respects me when I am not around."

Don Vito Corleone, The Godfather

Respect was and remains the highest of qualities revered by all Italians. It is a word that flies around amongst Sicilians during conversations, arguments and while disciplining children. We were taught at a very young age to respect our parents, elders, the family, authority and most importantly, ourselves.

Respect meant we spoke in appropriate tones, with kind words and gestures. Manners and being polite were also how we demonstrated respect. If we disrespected ourselves by misbehaving publicly, it was a poor reflection on the family.

To this day, I always greet my mom, my family and, really, most everybody with a kiss on the cheek. Failing to do so, especially with my mom's *cummari* (girlfriends), would not be nice. If you slight someone by not extending a proper greeting, you would be either reprimanded or become the topic of conversation.

> *"The Golden Rule!! Overall the significance of always showing respect!"*
>
> Lisa Ricci

Sicilians not only respect one another, they respect their environments, especially the home. Keeping a clean and tidy home is a must. Even when it came to cooking, cleaning up was tantamount to eating. This was drilled into my head:

> Mom: *"What's the most important part of cooking?"*
> My sister and I: *"Cleaning up!"*

The idea of respect actually encompasses every aspect of life. When you are respectful, you are mindful of yourself, the people with whom you interact and your environment. From respect flows all of the virtues: appreciation, love of neighbor, good citizenship, integrity, honesty, humility, responsibility, compassion,

forgiveness and loyalty, to name a few. I dive into some of these in future chapters.

Respect is one of the cornerstones of Sicilian living; the dinner table is the other. The benefit of showing respect is being respected in turn. However, behaving respectfully, regardless of others' behavior, is imperative. If you are wondering why kids are beating up their teachers, people walk away while you are speaking and your co-workers leave the break room a disaster, please know they have not been taught respect.

Applications

Family

The way to teach respect to your family is to be respectful. My children saw me speak kindly with grocery store employees, offer water to repairmen and bring Christmas cookies to the pediatrician. When I brought friends to my home as a kid, the first order of business was to find my parents and be sure my company said hello. My mother lost her marbles when our bedroom was a disaster. Her methods of getting us to clean may not have been ideal, but I definitely learned how to organize and respect my home. Here are some ideas to foster respect in your family:

- Treat everyone you meet with manners.
- Look people in the eyes during conversations, and demand that your children do the same.
- Greet your children and their friends when you walk into the house or room. Your children should do the same for you.
- Spend time with grandparents and older folks.

- Keep hotel rooms orderly. When visiting friends for an overnight, make your bed and keep your accommodations tidy.
- Speak respectfully about people in authority like teachers, police officers, firemen, the mayor, etc. (Side note: This is not a political statement. You can explain wrongdoing to your kids without disrespecting the office. You are an authority figure to your kids. They will not always agree with you, and in fact they may never agree with you. However, they must respect you and treat you properly. Do the same for authority figures.)
- Clean your kitchen, and if you do not know how to cook, now is the time to learn.

Life

Respecting yourself demonstrates to others that you honor your worth. Choosing behaviors that embrace self-respect teaches those around you how to regard you. How you dress, the words you select to describe yourself and your actions are cues that you expect to be treated accordingly. Knowing your worth and respecting yourself is the foundation for establishing healthy boundaries.

Respecting your boundaries and others' boundaries fosters healthy relationships. Healthy relationships are respectful. A tribe that is respectful is a supportive loving community. Using manners with your friends shows them you care about them as well as yourself. Here's how to foster respectful relationships:

- Look people in the eyes when conversing.
- Treat people how you would like to be treated.
- Be kind to waiters, the valet, and store clerks whether you are alone, on a date or with your crew.

- If you feel you have been disrespected, have that tough conversation. If it continues, it is time to question the relationship.
- Keep a tidy home and car.
- At work, clean up your office or desk and the break room after you use it.
- Are you still texting?

In Business

Everyone wants to feel valuable. They want to know they are heard. By demonstrating respect in the workplace, you will help people to feel appreciated. They will be happier, more productive and take less sick days. The benefits of a respectful workplace are infinite and will positively affect the bottom line. Here are some ways to show and teach respect in the workplace:

- Say good morning; greet people every day!
- Encourage co-workers to express new ideas and use the suggestions whenever possible.
- Disagreements happen; communicate using kind words, tone of voice and body language and reciprocate by listening.
- Do not allow insults or name calling.
- Be inclusive, not exclusive.
- Treat everyone fairly.
- Hire someone like me to teach you and your co-workers how to be respectful.
- Be excited to see your work family every day!

Like Glue

"Never rat on your friends and always keep your mouth shut."

Goodfellas

From the womb of respect is birthed loyalty. Sicilians are loyal to a fault with family, friends and fellow *paesani*. We were taught to keep our eyes open and our mouths shut. We stand by and behind our friends and family.

This does not mean we need to agree with everything. Some things are up for discussion, and others, well, not so much. Even if there is an all-out war going on behind closed doors, to the world, we are a united brood. We stand by each other through thick and thin, and we never let anyone outside the family know what is really happening.

> *"Never tell anyone outside the Family what you are thinking again."*
> *Don Vito Corleone, The Godfather*

For me, "The Family" includes my extended family, very close friends and of course my father's *cumpari* and my mother's *cummari*. Loyalty to these folks is second nature. We have always had each other's backs and still do.

> *"Don't trust people who tell you other people's secrets."*
> *Don Vito Corleone, The Godfather*

Loyalty in action is sticking up for your friend who is being bullied in the playground, never allowing someone to speak poorly about someone in your "family" and keeping private information to yourself. By living loyalty, I came to understand those less-than-admirable qualities to watch out for. People who gossip about others will gossip about you. Folks who stand by and watch their *paesani* being mistreated will not have the backbone to stick by you when the going gets tough. Fair-weather friends are just that; they are "Good Time Charlie's" who split when your road is a little rocky.

Being born with a rare disorder, Poland Syndrome, put me at an advantage when learning and teaching loyalty. My friends were there to protect me when I was mistreated and left out due to my limb difference. My cousins were especially loving to me. When my kids witnessed someone being mistreated in school, they knew I would blow a gasket if they did not stand up for their classmate. When my son Sean was part of a fraternity at The University of Alabama, a potential pledge with a limb difference visited the frat house. His fraternity brothers did not want to invite him to pledge. Sean spoke up for that boy, making me proud.

Loyalty has all but disappeared. Much like respect, adults are not loyal, and they do not teach it to their children. Your "best friend" will leave you alone at a nightclub, and your significant other is still active on Tinder. Employees are not loyal to their

bosses or companies. Companies make it clear that their staff are replaceable. Everyone wants to feel safe. Surrounding ourselves with folks who will not abandon or reject us no matter how bad it gets provides us security. Loyalty fosters feelings of confidence knowing we can turn around without having a knife stuck in our backs. Nobody likes going it alone. Being loyal and having loyal peeps around is a sign we are part of something bigger than ourselves: a family, friend group, company, or team.

Applications

Family

At the very least, one should be able to rely on one's family for loyalty. The family is where loyalty begins. Living the attribute of loyalty teaches children who to trust. It also becomes clearer from whom to walk away. Siblings will end up taking care of each other when adults are not around, even if it seems like they are always fighting. Kids will also know to whom they can go with problems or concerns. You can start to teach loyalty to your family anytime, but the earlier, the better.

- Parent as a team; present a united front.
- Allow children to be part of appropriate conversations with house guests.
- Tell stories that demonstrate loyalty.
- Insist that siblings take care of each other outside the home.
- Do not gossip with or in front of your kids.
- Use events at school or on the news as examples of where loyalty would have been beneficial.
- Be loyal yourself!

- Hire someone like me to teach you more about loyalty!
- If you do not know how to cook, now is the time to learn, so you can discuss loyalty at the dinner table!

Life

The world can be a scary place if we feel alone with nobody in our corner. Like all the other attributes in this book, you will receive what you give out; like attracts like. Nowadays, most people are fickle, ambivalent, opportunistic and basically self-serving. They are wishy-washy, spineless and adhere to whatever is the current popular belief. Loyalty calls for just the opposite: taking a stand for beliefs, friends and yourself, protecting that which is important in life. If the people in your world are less than loyal, who can you trust?

- Find good people and stick by them.
- Be sincere and caring.
- Respect other people's boundaries.
- Offer good, honest, solid advice to your friends.
- Call it like you see it; the truth will set you free, and sometimes it hurts.
- Be trustworthy, reliable and committed.
- Look for these qualities in others.
- You can hear loyalty in someone's voice, not over texts.
- Hire someone like me to help you with loyalty.

In Business

Creating a company where loyalty is the norm has to start from the top. When an employee knows their boss is behind them, they will go out on a limb for the company, co-workers and management. Imagine an entire staff, whether one employee or one thousand, that loves their job. They will tell their friends and family. This is free advertisement, folks! Your most valuable assets are the people with whom you share your work week. Here's how to foster a loyal workforce:

- Treat everyone like family (Go back and read chapter 1).
- Have your employees' backs.
- Listen to feedback, even if it is not exactly what you want to hear.
- Be the fall guy in the event there is an error or mistake: don't play the blame game!
- Do not criticize anybody publicly.
- Support your team in private and public.
- Always have others' best interest at heart.
- Hire the right people, give them their space and they will produce.
- Encourage supporting one another.
- Never tell or make anybody feel that they are replaceable, EVER!
- Hire someone like me to teach you and your co-workers loyalty.

Bless Me, For I Have Sinned

"Don't overestimate the power of forgiveness."
Michael Corleone, Godfather III

Forgiveness is not the first virtue that comes to mind when thinking about Sicilians. Hollywood shows us cement shoes and getting whacked for going against the family. I suppose in the rough underworld, this may occur, but this is not my experience growing up Sicilian. I know only love and forgiveness.

My family and our friends are all hot-headed, passionate, outspoken and opinionated folks who struggle holding their tongues. There are a hundred different reasons why my sister and I could not be speaking. I have been corrected more than once by my besties for my behavior. The whole lot of us would be eating Christmas Dinner alone if we did not forgive one another.

Sometimes I have had to let things go. I cared more about the relationship than being right. Being right all the time is a lonely place (even if you are right!). I could speak volumes about forgiveness. We all know it releases us from negative energy and has other benefits. For the purposes of this book, for Sicilians, forgiveness is about relationships. It is about holding on to those people who matter the most to us.

Every one of us has a bad day, week, month, or, Hell, year. We have all spoken out of turn, without knowing all the facts, and made false assumptions. We have pointed the finger; turned our nose up or back on the people we love most. Those closest to us are usually the ones who bear the brunt of our pain. These are the ones who know us best. They can tell us where we went wrong. They welcome us back after we lost our marbles to a warm loving family. You just might have to endure wisecracks at the table. It is all worth it for the peace of mind that you are loved and accepted.

There are several ways to navigate hurtful situations where one or both parties need forgiving. One way is having a tough conversation. One thing I have done with my children and my friends is I give them fifteen minutes to tell me whatever they want about me and my behavior. This is scary. You listen. Then take your fifteen minutes to tell your side. Most of the time people merely need to be heard, and the guard will come down. After hearing each other, discuss solutions, apologize and offer ways to avoid the situations that brought you here. Know if you go so far as to even ask for this conversation, this person is probably worth keeping around. Read below for suggestions on how to incorporate forgiveness into your relationships:

Applications

Family

When I consider forgiveness and family, I want to say, "Really?" Do we need to even teach about forgiveness in families? Do you need a slap on your forehead? Who holds a grudge with their children?" Unfortunately it happens.

Forgiveness in families is imperative. Are you going to throw your four-year-old out after he climbs on the counter and starts digging through the beautifully decorated cake you made to serve your mom for her 80th birthday? The family is the first teacher of forgiveness. Forgiveness is not the welcome wagon for bad or disrespectful behavior. It is the catalyst that strengthens interpersonal bonds. It is experienced and observed. The kids are not the only ones who make mistakes. Believe me, I have had to eat crow with my kids. Tips to open communication when feelings and egos are bruised:

- Allow your kids to observe you forgiving other adults, a teaching moment.
- Ask for forgiveness from your children, we all screw up, and more than a few times.

- Learn from your children. Kids are naturally forgiving. They care more about you and your relationship than holding grudges.
- When your kids are in hot water, communicate. Avoid the silent treatment and spinning your head around and vomiting pea soup. Tell them you forgive them.
- Practice forgiveness everywhere. This energy will be felt by your family.
- Hire someone like me to help you understand forgiveness and how to practice it in your life.
- If you do not know how to cook, now is the time to learn! The dinner table is a great place to discuss forgiveness.

Life

Forgiveness is a two-way street in all relationships. Often we are the schmucks who seek forgiveness after a night of nasty drunk texts (been there!). How many times have our feelings been hurt by a slight from our bestie? Being right all the time is a lonely place. Asking for forgiveness and forgiving others strengthens bonds and releases us from exerting unnecessary negative energy that only breeds more misery.

In the forgiveness arena, we need to look at who has wronged us and decide if the relationship or being right is more important. Often, we are the ones who hurt others. Do we want to lose people and maintain our pride? Eating crow and owning up to our less-than-admirable behavior is not only good for our own humility, apologizing keeps the people we cherish in our lives.

Know you are one nasty comment away from never talking to someone again, including family. This does not mean you need to fear losing people. Having empathy and some self-restraint in difficult situations can salvage a worthy relationship. This has taken me years to practice. Sicilians are not known for keeping quiet. However, we will forgive people because we know next go-around we may need the forgiveness. In Sicily there is a saying: *"Chi ha un culo lo sa."* Translated: "He who has an ass knows."

Tips for incorporating forgiveness with your tribe:

- Know when to stay quiet. (Umm, yup, I need to do this too!)
- Learn how to have difficult conversations.
- Listen more; talk less.
- Write a letter or email asking for forgiveness.
- Get confident, not just comfortable, in your own skin. When you are secure, your happiness will not depend on the actions of others. Stay off someone else's emotional roller coaster.
- Be proactive: when you are harboring negative energy, thoughts and feelings, think twice about going out. Stay home and watch Law & Order SVU until you can offer more to your friends.
- Let things go. Know on which hill you want to die. The rest is meaningless. You know the cliché, "Don't sweat the small stuff." In other words, have nothing to forgive because people's moods, drunk comments and forgetfulness don't rock your boat.
- Drunk texting is a no-no!
- Hire someone like me to help you release resentments.

Business:

Employees, co-workers, business partners and owners are all human. They come to work after dealing with who knows what at home. They get sick, hungry, angry, lonely and tired.

There needs to be some level of emotional intelligence in the workplace. When mistakes are made, understanding where the person is at emotionally and why they made their choices will aid in the forgiving process.

Of course, it is understandable to let someone go when they are not invested in the growth and well-being of the company. Eventually these unhappy folks will stand out. When an employee or co-worker has a negative attitude, consistently complains and makes errors that hurt the bottom line, it is imperative to rectify this situation, even if it results in firing someone. These are extreme cases.

Spending forty hours or more a week with anybody can be annoying at one point or another. Unless it is a family business, people come from all kinds of upbringings. After college, I worked in corporate America. To me, people were nuts. I was relatively new to the non-Sicilian world. I worked with a lady who did not look you in the eye when you spoke to her. I felt like slapping her and saying in my mother's tone of voice, "Look at me when I talk to you!" I had to forgive her for being rude every day.

Fostering a forgiving atmosphere at work will provide a safe environment for creativity to flow. People will not be afraid to take risks, share new ideas and communicate effectively. Here are some ways to implement forgiveness at work:

- If you are the boss, apologize when you make a mistake.
- Ask for forgiveness.
- When an employee or co-worker hurts your feelings or someone else's, sit down with them and ask them if they would like to share what is going on in their lives.
- Make light of situations that are not worth the energy. Let stuff go!

- Take the heat when someone on your team messes up externally. After all, you chose the team. If a client or customer is unhappy, be the fall guy. Then deal with it internally.
- If your business is a family gig, be nice! It is easier to be mean or insensitive to those who are closest to you.
- Hire someone like me to come in and give a "lunch and learn" on forgiveness.

The Shirt Off My Back

"I'm gonna make him an offer he can't refuse."
Don Corleone (Marlon Brando),
The Godfather

Sicilians are a generous bunch. My father would give a bottle of Galliano to Mike the Mailman every Christmas. My Nana handed out hot cocoa in the winter and cups of water in the summer to the garbage men. I have literally given one of my girlfriends my blouse I was wearing after she told me she loved it. We give money to the church, even if we do not go, make a lasagne for our neighbor who just had her fifth baby and leave a turkey dinner at the homeless shelter at Thanksgiving.

My uncle Inzy would slip me five dollars and tell me I was his favorite. He told me not to tell my sister. Then he did the same with her. Until my grandmother died, she mailed me ten dollars on my birthday. I was 41 when she passed away.

Generosity actually is born from gratitude. I am going to take a short gratitude detour here. Sicilians, especially grandmas and older folks, are always thanking God when things work out, a new baby is born and when cousin Joey makes it to Sunday dinner. When I told Grandma I was pregnant with my last baby, she shouted, "Thank God, finally some good news!" I should tell you here that I always struggled to call Grandma when I was pregnant because now she knew what I had been doing. In other words, be thankful for all that you have, and generosity will flow.

> "I love the generosity of Sicilians; their art of sharing is second to none. Wander through the colorful fish market in Catania and you will be inundated with offers of tastes of fresh shrimp; in the delicatessens of Syracuse you can sample cheese, olives and flavorsome salami; in the bars in Palermo and Taormina the bartenders are so welcoming, giving complementary bowls of olives, bite-sized hot pizza and other spicy bar snacks to enjoy with your wine."
>
> Dominique Rizzo

Generosity is a virtue that does not have to include money. Being generous with your time, lending an ear and driving your friend to pick up her car that she left at the valet last night all count. My grandfather would drive to Cape Cod to pick me up; remember, no cell phones or GPS in those days. My father would go to Chinatown to pick up a decent egg roll for us. Nobody ever said they were too busy to help.

Sicilians will drop everything on a dime if their friend calls and needs help moving a piece of furniture, building a retaining wall or constructing an outdoor pizza oven. For Sicilians, friends are family, and family are friends. My Sicilian friend Ciccio is always taking a sick friend to the doctor, comforting someone who lost a loved one and restoring homes with his brother-in-law, all out of the generosity in his heart. While I was out of town, my friend, Jeff, installed dimmers on all my lights all while checking on my place and taking a nap on my couch.

"Being proud of being Sicilian and letting people know how giving we are by sharing my love of the food, even while living in Alabama where most people had no clue what it meant to be a Sicilian."

Viola Nicosia

One evening while I was living in Atlanta, I had my mom and two of my young boys in my car. My gas tank was on empty and I was in a very rough area of town. I pulled into the gas station where many homeless people were trying to get warm. While pumping gas, I was approached by a homeless man (my mom almost fainted). He asked me for a blanket. I happened to have six blankets in my car for an outdoor event we had just attended. I gave him two blankets. He immediately wrapped himself up. I was a bit nervous, but he needed the blankets. My kids recall this story to this day.

Generosity is a spirit. Being generous will attract abundance in your life and make the people in your world feel included, cared for and special. Just like gratitude, incorporate generosity in your daily life.

Applications

Family

Have you ever met an adult who came from a stingy family? They covet everything they have out of fear that they will lose it or someone will take it away. This why we teach our children to share. A marriage that lacks in generosity is a dark one indeed. Some ways to become a generous family:

- Start teaching your kids to be grateful by being grateful yourself and demonstrating appreciation for them and everything in your lives.
- Be an example of generosity: donate cupcakes (even store bought) to the bake sale at school; offer a cold drink to repair people who come to fix something at your home; drive other kids home from practice and give little tokens of appreciation to your spouse.
- Give undivided attention to your family members when they need you; put down the phone!
- Encourage sharing between siblings.
- Host their friends for dinners. This is a good time to learn how to cook, if you do not know already!
- If you have disposable income, give to philanthropic endeavors, church, local animal shelters.
- Volunteer with your family at orphanages (this will teach them gratitude for sure), nursing homes, animal shelters, etc.
- Hire someone like me to teach you how to be grateful and generous without breaking the bank.

Life

Hopefully you were taught gratitude and shown generosity. If so, it will be much easier for you to be generous. We live in a world today where we keep blinders on. I am not suggesting you be a doormat or an ATM. We mind our business when it comes to helping a stranger, and we are stingy with our time and money out of fear that someone is going to take advantage of our kindness. This is conditional love, only giving when you will get something in return. Cut this out right now! Here's how:

- Invite people who never entertain to your home for dinner or coffee.
- Help the elderly woman next door unload her groceries. Ask if you can do an errand for her.
- Offer to drive your friend to the airport.
- Listen wholeheartedly when someone needs to vent.
- A phone call is more effort than texting; it's a sign of generosity. Call your mom, sister, whomever to ask how they are doing.
- Hire someone like me to teach you how to be grateful and generous.

Business

As an employer, you can be the shining example of generosity for your troop. An office filled with grateful, caring, generous individuals will greatly benefit the bottom line. Co-workers who give to each other will trust each other. You will find folks who finished their work "to do" list assisting others instead of surfing the internet. Generous people care about the well-being of others. In the workplace, helping with projects, resolving client issues and concerns will become everyone's responsibility. They will rely on each other instead of isolating themselves, fearing their job may be in jeopardy.

- Get to know your employees and co-workers.
- Offer to help out with projects.
- Offer to drive a co-worker home whose car is in the shop.
- Adopt or start a charity. Make one Friday afternoon a quarter volunteer time for that charity.
- Assign one day per month as the day to celebrate that month's birthdays. Have a cake, put balloons at their desks or make a donation to a charity in their name.
- Be available after hours in the event a co-worker needs a friend to lend an ear or a shoulder.
- Be happy to give!
- Hire someone like me to come in and teach generosity to your crew.

They Work Hard For Their Money

"Listen to me very carefully. There are three ways of doing things around here: the right way, the wrong way, and the way that I do it. You understand?"

Ace Rothstein (Robert DeNiro), Casino

If you travel to Sicily, it may seem as though nobody works. Men gather at the coffee bars to talk in the mornings, and spending time with beloved friends and family is a daily occurrence. As you immerse yourself in the culture, you will experience the joy that Sicilians exude when you dine at their restaurant or purchase original works of art at local shops.

Sicilians are a very proud people. They are dedicated to their work. Whatever their craft, for Sicilians, it is a work of art.

It is their purpose, their gift to give to the world. In Sciacca, a small town on the south side of Sicily, you can walk into any of the ceramic stores and watch the artist paint tiles, statues and pottery. Chefs and bakers love to talk to their guests and offer samples of their delicacies.

> *"I just want to be an evennaire."*
>
> *Mikey Zarba*, during a conversation about millionaires.

In Sicily, they work for just enough money to make ends meet. They do what they do because they love it. They are excited and thrilled to talk about their work. The small pasta shop is the best. You can walk in and tell them what you are planning to cook. They will tell you the best pasta and how much you will need, all freshly made, of course.

> *"Trying your best at work because, 'Whatever you do reflects not just on you, but also on our family.' I still remember that conversation."*
>
> *Richard De Francesco*

Carpenters, fishermen, winemakers, restaurateurs, farmers and seamstresses all live each day with the purpose of giving back to the world the very gifts given to them. Without thinking or consideration, they automatically tap into their strengths and gifts in their unique businesses. They work from sunup to sundown, with siesta, of course. The pride they take in their work is a reflection on their upbringing and the family, especially if they are running a family business.

> *"Hard work, because my grandfather had me working when I was seven years old!"*
>
> Paul Oliva

How can you be deeply proud of your work if you hate your job? Sicilian are creative. Everything they do is a reflection of their alignment to themselves, God and the people they serve. The only way to get to this place is to understand your purpose, gifts and what you truly love to do. Perhaps you studied accounting because you are good at math. However, you spend all your free time painting canvases. Time flies when you are creating masterpieces all weekend, and you still cannot believe it is only 10:30 a.m. Monday morning when you are at your accounting job. This is not a purpose-driven career.

> *"There's no such thing as good money or bad money. There's just money".*
>
> Lucky Luciano

Imagine a world where people recognize and own their gifts. Think of a world where those people make a living tapping into their strengths, gifts and purpose. Nobody would be working a day in their lives. It could be a happy, balanced world! It could happen. How do we get there and still be able to afford to feed ourselves and our families? Glad you asked. As an aside, I believe in that world where everyone is happy. You may think I believe in fairy tales. Yup, I do!

Applications

Family

The family is where it starts. When my children were very young, my husband (now ex-husband and not a Sicilian) came home from work and told me he wanted to start his own design-build construction company. He planned on partnering with a sub-contractor for some time while he built the general contracting business. He was going to have to take a thirty-thousand dollar a year pay cut. I told him to do it. I knew he was tired of working his ass off for someone else. I also knew it was in his blood. He needed to do this. I supported his efforts and gave as much as I could to host dinners and parties for employees, vendors and clients. He grew his company into an international business living his purpose.

Although the father of my children, yes the one I supported, opposed everything I tried to teach my kids, I took every chance I got to tell my kids to do what makes them happy. I encouraged them to travel before settling into a marriage. If they were struggling during college, I insisted they get their lives in order then go back to school. It does not matter how old you are when you graduate. Who cares if you are 22 or 25 when you walk to receive your diploma?

I believe if we can get parents to live their purpose and teach it to their children, we will have the world I described a few paragraphs above. Here's what you can do:

- Work on yourself. Practice self-care. Get aligned with yourself, your higher power and the universe. Discover your purpose, your passions, what floats your boat.

- Live that purpose. If it is not possible to make a profitable business out of it, make it your main hobby. This can be your time to reset and recharge.
- Talk to your kids about your hopes, goals and your passions.
- Encourage your partner to do the same.
- Watch your kids. Catch them doing what makes them the happiest. Talk to them about it.
- Offer inside and outside school activities that they love.
- Get creative. Have kids who love talking about sports statistics start a club in school (colleges love this, by the way!). Encourage them to join groups or clubs that teach them more about their passion like a film editing class for the kid who loves to use his GoPro, etc.
- Tell them to do what they love. Ask them if they could do anything in the world, what would they do?
- Make this a topic over dinner!
- Hire someone like me to help you find your purpose and to advise you on bringing this school of thought to your family.

Life

I believe we all can be successful by creating or finding a career where we are living our purpose and gifts every day. I know we can take what we are passionate about and make enough money to live comfortable lives. Often we end up choosing our professions because we think it will bring us success, and we end up twenty years into it and miserable. It is the supernatural gifts embedded in who we are that bring us joy when put to use.

I earned a Bachelor of Arts with a major in Management and a certificate in Communications. I proceeded to stay home to raise my boys for 20 years. I always knew I was meant for more. I wanted to help people understand themselves. I always wanted to be excited to be me and show others the way to experience the same. It took me 48 years and a painful divorce to start digging deeper. Do not wait that long! Be passionate today. Do what you love and never work a day for the rest of your life:

- Surround yourself with like-minded people who continue to evolve.
- At work, recognize tasks that utilize your gifts and offer to tackle them.
- If you cannot leave your boring job due to finances, either take up a hobby that brings a smile to your face or start a side hustle.
- Walk away from or keep at arm's length any people who do not support you, ridicule you or become obstacles to your personal advancement. This may mean limiting time with family and friends from the old 'hood who still use "Dippity Do" and "Aqua Net" in their hair.
- Read good books.
- Engage in face to face intellectual conversations with folks in your tribe who have the capacity to do so.
- Hire someone like me to help you identify your purpose and muster the courage to live it.

Business

Because the topic is basically finding your labor of love, my hope is that business owners reading this book are running companies that have been born from their gifts, passions and purpose. If you do not fall into this group and you own a company that you either dislike or about which you are ambivalent, well, I feel sorry for you. For those bosses and managers who are living their dreams, here are some ways you can help employees tap into theirs:

- Be proactive. Be a strengths-based organization. Hire people whose shining abilities fit the role you are filling.
- Ask each person on your team what they really love to do. To the best of your ability, assign projects that correspond to those passions. You will have a happier crew!
- Again, take the time to get to know your staff. Have conversations, engage in activities outside the office and adopt some of the practices mentioned in the first two chapters of this book.
- Do NOT focus on weaknesses. Merely hire someone else whose strengths make up for another's shortcomings.
- Put someone like me on retainer to guide all your employees toward a purpose-driven life and how to apply that at work. On a smaller scale, bring me in for a "lunch and learn" on aligning and identifying your gifts.

Put On the Coffee

"Funny how? You mean funny like I'm a clown, I amuse you?"

Tommy DeVito (Joe Pesci), GoodFellas

Remember the days when family friends would show up at your door unannounced? I do! My aunt would call and say, "Steph, tell your mother to put on the coffee, I'm coming ovaah." We enjoyed Sunday dinners with extended family and friends all day into the evening. Christmas Day was nonstop eating, and my mother should have installed a revolving door.

Americans have lost something through the years. Certainly millennials fill their leisure time with jumping out of airplanes and hours of Fortnite. I guess that could be fun for some, but my best times are those when I am with my family and friends laughing until it hurts. Inevitably, whatever I am drinking starts coming out of my nose. Then we all laugh harder. Nothing can replace leisure time with the people we love and cherish.

"Living happens during leisure. That's where the body is refreshed, the heart is moved, the spirit is lifted and the mind expanded."

Just Steph

Sicilians thrive on leisure time. They gather in the piazza to have coffee, eat or enjoy an evening cocktail. Their nights evolve into early morning conversations at a local coffee bar. When I was in Terrasini, Sicily, we would inevitably wind up going for coffee after a nightclub. I found myself looking at my phone shocked to see that it was 4:00 a.m.! I also hosted dinners with between 10 and 15 Sicilians at my table. They never left, and I was so happy. I did not want the night to end. I spent wonderful days resting on the beach at San Vito Lo Capo and evenings strolling around town with my dear friends.

When I returned to America from Sicily, I decided I was going to enjoy my leisure time with those who wanted to stop and smell the roses with me. As soon as my condominium just north of Boston was renovated, I began hosting Sunday dinners for my family and closest friends. I open my home to my married friends, single peeps and business associates. I also decided that my personal time was sacred. I want to laugh, learn and breathe. Therefore, I choose my activities and company wisely expecting to fill my soul, lift my spirits and expand my mind with the folks who are dancing to that same beat.

My heart longs to return to Sicily because although I took much of the thought processes back with me, it is so easy to slip back into a solitary, chaotic, rushed way of living. We all need to continue practicing and living what we preach. I want the best part of the Sicilian lifestyle to become second nature to me. Hanging with my peeps, either here or in Sicily, spending fun, quality time with my tribe makes my life more than happy.

My leisure time, as yours should be, is where my personal relationships are strengthened. These are the folks who get us through the rough patches in life. Do not waste one minute of your leisure time on frivolous, meaningless nothingness. Learn to choose leisure, and choose how you fill it wisely.

Applications

Family

The first thought that comes to mind when merging leisure time with family is vacations. While family vacations are a great way to bond, they are costly and time consuming. If you can afford it, take an annual trip with the entire family. A car trip can be daunting in a packed minivan, and it can be fun depending on everyone's attitude. Getting on an airplane and heading to Disney or an all-inclusive family-friendly resort on an island is a blast as well.

Families do not have to go anywhere to bond during leisure time. My mother hosted my entire family, cousins, aunts, uncles, every Friday night for years. Inevitably we would all play the card game Crazy Eights. My uncle Joe earned the title "Crazy Joe" after beating us all in a tournament that lasted hours and hours. My cousins and I would sit on the swing at my grandmother's and laugh about nothing. Here's how to make the most out of family leisure time:

- Carve out time for activities. Let everyone know that Saturday the entire fam is headed to the park to play kickball. Let the kids invite their friends, or bring cousins along.
- Ban technology from family time. Today's kids do not know how to play Monopoly or Clue.

- Invite extended family to your home for coffee and dessert.
- Do dinner and a movie together.
- Make your holidays a priority. Include the people closest to you to participate in your celebrations.
- For one-on-one time, take one of your children on a date. Go to dinner and a museum or the mall.
- Be an example, spend quality time with your spouse and friends.
- Do not allow anyone to leave the dinner table until the conversations are exhausted.
- Hire someone like me to help you figure out how to reap the most from your leisure time for yourself and your family.

Life

If you are single and you do not have children, you may find yourself with more leisure time than you want. You may also be the type who joins every social club in town to circumvent loneliness. Most of my Sicilian friends, those living in Sicily, are single. Many of those folks are very young. However, because they were raised in the small villages outside of Palermo, they were raised with the old school values. They definitely frequent nightclubs until four in the morning, but they spend hours on end talking with their friends.

I was shocked when I invited my young Sicilian friends for dinner, and they stayed enjoying food and drink for hours all while chatting incessantly. Nobody refused the invitations, put time limits on their visits or were at all bored for all those hours. Conversely, I was included in Sunday dinners at their homes that lasted eight or nine hours. The bottom line is: I was forging and building relationships.

It is those relationships that evoked my understanding that this is how I fill my cup. My needs were being met by my leisure time. For those of you who are growing your tribe, here are some things you can do to ensure every moment of your leisure feeds your soul:

- Choose activities that interest you and that you love.
- Include your friends in those activities.
- Take vacations from work.
- Sneak a siesta in over the weekends.
- Purchase cards with questions to break the ice. Invite friends for dinner and pull out the cards as conversation starters.
- Sit on the beach with a friend for a few hours.
- For the record, Facebook Messenger is the same as texting.

Business

Work and leisure appear juxtaposed. I agree you cannot play ping pong all day at the office and expect to make a profit. However, by encouraging your team to engage in healthy leisure activities, you will have a more relaxed, satisfied work family. A happy workplace is a more productive and profitable business. A company that exceeds revenue goals can offer more bonuses, leisure activities, and perks...all of which make everyone even happier.

The idea of leisure is to recharge and avoid burnout. Many people are burning the candle at both ends. Their time off of work may be spent engaging in draining activities, like hauling kids around, yard work, or caregiving for an ailing parent. As their boss, you can offer your staff suggestions on how to spend at least some of their non-working hours. Here are some leisure suggestions:

- Engage in the outside of work activities mentioned in the first two chapters of this book.
- Get a ping pong table.
- If possible, offer gym memberships as a perk, or convert one of your larger offices into a small fitness room.
- Bring everyone bowling after work one day and include pizza and beer.
- Start a co-ed softball team and join a local league.
- Encourage your team to take their vacation time. You need them to take this break.
- I offered this in Chapter Two, "Pass the Pasta." It is worth mentioning again here. Host dinners at your home. You will notice a major attitude adjustment in your staff. I promise!
- Hire someone like me to help you implement leisure activities and encourage healthy leisure at your place of business.

Don't Be A Scaredy Cat

"No matter how big a guy might be, Nicky would take him on. You beat Nicky with fists, he comes back with a bat. You beat him with a knife, he comes back with a gun. And you beat him with a gun, you better kill him, because he'll keep comin' back and back until one of you is dead."
Robert DeNiro as Ace Rothstein, Casino

Sicilian mothers are always worried their kid is going to get hit by a car, struck by lightning or catch Ebola. When it comes to their children, Sicilians will worry until they are too old to remember what they were worried about. With that said, Sicilians are not afraid of anything. If they are, you will never know it.

My family used to spend weekends at my aunt's cottage in Wareham, MA. While that small house on Repose Lane comfortably slept six people, on any given weekend there were at least twenty of us sleeping wall to wall on cots. We even slept in cars one time. Inevitably we woke up on Sunday morning every weekend to the smell of Nana Josephine's (my aunt's mother, not my blood relative, but family, nonetheless) meatballs frying and the sauce boiling.

On one of those weekends, the entire family, except Nana Josephine who was back at the cottage cooking, was at the lake. While all of the kids were digging rivers in the sand or drowning each other in the lake, our parents were on lounge chairs relaxing to the sounds of the seventies song "Heaven Must Be Missing an Angel" by Tavares. There were other folks on the beach. A man close by to my uncle complained about something insignificant. My uncle ignored him. He persisted and my uncle told that man he felt like putting the radio through his face. That man was a Massachusetts State Trooper.

Later, what seemed to be the entire police force showed up at the cottage. My uncle was arrested. He never actually hit the guy nor did he get up off his chair. My uncle never flinched even when he was cuffed. We all went to court and my uncle beat the charge. The whole time, my uncle never backed down. At eighty years old today, he would not even feel or show fear.

I have witnessed many events like this. I use the example of a near-physical altercation to prove a point. What is important to understand is fear holds us back from expressing who we are, what we stand for and how we will go about getting what is ours. Fear cripples us. Most of our fears are buried deep in our subconscious. They hold us back from taking a new job, asking someone out on a date, starting our own businesses, making new friends.

"Keep your friends close, but your enemies closer."
Al Pacino as Michael Corleone,
The Godfather II

We do not have to engage in fights with baseball bats or threaten people to prove our courage. We have to muster up the fearlessness of Sicilians who would take a bullet for someone they love, protect their friends and live their lives with conviction and integrity. This includes Sicilian women. Have you ever teased a Sicilian kid? Watch what happens when their mother finds out. You are going down and so is your mother. It will probably be a verbal assault, but do not be shocked that she may be holding her broom.

As a Sicilian-American living with a limb difference my entire life, I was always afraid that someone was going to ridicule my hand. Later, as an adult, that fear morphed into fear of public humiliation. I had to reach deep down and connect with my Sicilian roots. I released this fear in order to live my best life, write my books, work with clients and audiences all while owning my gifts of empathy and healing.

> *"You don't make up for your sins in church. You do it in the streets. You do it at home."*
>
> Martin Scorsese as the
> narrator, Mean Streets

There is no space in my life for fear if I want to be successful and happy. I encourage you to face your fears, look them straight in the eye and whack them in the knees with your baseball bat like a good Sicilian!

Applications

Family

The family is the best place to be proactive. Whether you realize it or not, you are forming the subconscious of your children. Ninety-five to 99 percent of everything we do is fueled by our subconscious beliefs. We are on a treadmill, and, for the most part, we are merely floating through life without a conscious thought.

All the fears we have about rejection, abandonment, public humiliation, etc. are implanted in us at a very early age. Parents, siblings, extended family, childhood experiences and teachers shape our subconscious from the beginning. We really have very little control over most of the events that plant the fear seed deep into our minds. We can only look at ourselves and work at evolving into mindful, fearless humans. This example to your children will be your greatest tool in the healthy development of their young minds. Outside of kicking the neighborhood bully's ass, here are some pointers on growing into an emotionally healthy, aware family:

- Practice meditation and mindfulness.
- Face your greatest fears: accept that speaking gig or read at your church services. Start your own side hustle and support your partner's entrepreneurial endeavors.
- Encourage your children to run for class officer, start a club, try out for the team, take up a musical instrument.

- Be there when it does not work out for them. Validate their feelings.
- If they are victims of bullying or teasing, again, validate their feelings. Give reasons why their arch-enemy may be mean.
- Help your children to recognize their gifts and that they should use them for good, no matter how scary this may be.
- If necessary, find a good therapist for you and/or your children.
- Do not be afraid to try cooking. You can do it!
- Hire someone like me to help you uncover your subconscious fears, face and release them

Life

Operating out of fear is victim mentality. Fear is a powerless position. Somebody, something, some thought, some belief is steering your ship. You have relinquished the helm. You may not even realize it until it bites you in the ass. You cannot commit in a relationship. You avoid certain conversations. You crumble when someone calls you out on something you did. There are a million scenarios. The tell-tale signs that you are fearful is a turned stomach, shaking, tears, lump in your throat, even anger. You experience the physical feelings and emotions, but you are not exactly sure where the root is buried. Here is how to put on your big boy boxers and big girl panties:

- Meditate daily.
- Become aware of your physical reactions to situations.
- Journal; take notes on when you feel less than happy. Watch the pattern.

- Surround yourself with fearless friends. Watch how they forge ahead.
- Listen to your internal voice nudging you to step out of your comfort zone to try something new, and go for it.
- Take time to be alone. Be quiet. Breathe. This is where you will hear your inner being guiding you.
- You are not still texting, are you?
- If your fears are truly debilitating you, get into therapy.
- Hire someone like me to help you work through your fears.

Business

I am not sure if employers realize how truly afraid people are at work. Most people, at one time or another, fear losing their jobs if they make a mistake. Do not be shocked to realize your co-worker is afraid you are after his job. Your team members may be holding back on a fantastic idea that will attract clients and raise profits, but they are afraid to tell you because they are afraid you will steal their idea, or worse, tell them it is a ridiculous plan of action.

Business and fear seem juxtaposed, but they are actually in bed with each other. I believe every person on earth, whether at home, in school or at work, has the right to feel safe. Of course, we cannot possibly know about every individual's subconscious formation. We can however provide a safe environment at the office and with our teams.

For years I played cards once a month with a wonderful, fun group of ladies in Atlanta. We played at tables of four, pairs of two in each team. As we played and the discard pile grew, it was a risk to pick up the pile. You could end up deducting massive amounts of points from your team's total. For the most part, she who took the risk and picked up the pile won that round for her team. If you fear the pile, you may never win a round. Same goes in business. The risks will raise your profits. Pacify your staff's worry with some of the following fear busters:

- Have weekly or monthly brainstorming meetings. All ideas are welcome and valid no matter how bizarre.
- Sit down one-on-one with your team members and ask for feedback.
- Make it a company policy that all ideas and creativity will be received, even if it is not implemented.
- Encourage a spirit of teamwork. Do not accept any actions or words that belittle ideas.
- If you are a strengths-based organization, folks will be doing what they love and will have less fear of losing their jobs.
- Every individual is unique. No two people will do a job exactly the same way, and nobody is replaceable. If someone tried to tell you are replaceable, replace them! Make this known throughout your organization.
- Be understanding when an employee has an outside life issue: a new marriage, baby, death, divorce, a tree fell on their car, etc.
- Make sure each person feels welcome and appreciated.
- Hire someone like me to talk to your crew about the pitfalls of fear and the benefits of operating from the position of confidence in themselves.

'Til Death Do Us Part

"There is no need to seek love. If you be love, love will surround you."

Just Steph

It would not do anyone justice if I left out the most important aspect of being raised in a Sicilian home: love. Regardless of all the chaos, fights, screaming and crying in my home, I knew I was loved. Sicilians love like they do everything else: passionately. We love without fear or shame. Our greetings with a kiss are an outward sign of love and respect.

"When there's love, mountains seem like plains."
Sicilian Proverb

Love drives everything Sicilians think, feel and do. We love our children, our cousins, aunts, uncles, grandparents and friends to a fault. When it comes to romance, a true Sicilian

man will not let anything get in the way of his love for his woman. And as for Sicilian women, well, there is a saying in Sicily: "Women are more dangerous than shotguns."

We love our towns and villages. We are devoted to our work, family and friends. Sicilians give their love freely and without reservation. Emotions run wild when it comes to Sicilians loving their families or when we are in love. They love beyond death. Have you ever attended a Sicilian funeral? The crying, wailing and occasional screaming are the signs of a brokenhearted Sicilian.

The love we Sicilians have for ourselves, our families, work, traditions, food, wine and the old country is our raison d'être, our very reason for being. If we could all love like Sicilians, this world would be a much better place. Take a risk, be vulnerable share your heart and love always!

Applications

Family

Families exist because of love. You would be shocked at the number of adults who sense they were not loved as children. I cannot imagine how that must feel. We were always squeezed, pinched, hugged and kissed ad nauseam. My mother would scream, "I love her!" out of the clear blue. I would shout out during my son's football game, "Look at him! He's so handsome!" (As if everyone could tell what he looked like with his helmet on.)

C.S. Lewis names the love between parents and children "storge." It is understood as "cherishing one's kindred, especially parents or children and wives and husbands; loving affection; prone to love; loving tenderly; chiefly of the reciprocal tenderness of parents and children." Many people struggle telling their children and each other they love them. Some cannot hug or hold their loved ones. Whatever that is, if this describes you, you need to make some real changes. The way you show love at home perpetuates with your children. Time to break the generational curses! Here's how:

- Practice self-care. Loving others starts with yourself.
- Look in the mirror and say, "I love you." Do it!
- Show appropriate affection with your partner in front of the kids: kiss hello, goodbye, goodnight, etc.
- If your parents struggled with showing love, know they were not shown love themselves. Here's where you feel bad for them. By holding back love, you miss out on a beautiful part of life.
- Explain to your kids in private why grandma is not a big hugger. They will jump on the sympathy band wagon with you, when you are honest about your childhood.
- Hug your extended family and friends when appropriate. Hug your kids every day. I told my kids everybody needs twelve hugs a day to thrive. It doesn't matter if it is true or not. I get a hug out of them!

- Tell your kids you love them.
- Show your kids you love them by learning to cook and preparing family dinners.
- Hire someone like me to teach you to be able to give and receive love.

Life

If you can understand that love is the source of all creation, healing, well-being, happiness and even death, you are halfway there. Knowing this can fuel your desire to give and receive love at all levels. Love is meant to be given without seeking anything in return. Love should be received with an open heart.

Healthy love is expressed differently between family members, friends and romantic partners. The love we share with others is a reflection of the divine. As humans we fall short of divine love, agape in Greek. However, agape needs to be our goal, loving as Infinite Intelligence loves. Here's how to make love a priority in your life:

- Take care of yourself physically, emotionally, intellectually and spiritually. Self-care is imperative.
- Focus on the positive.
- Surround yourself with positive loving people.
- Heal fragmented relationships that are important to maintain.
- Walk away from toxic people and experiences, including family and family drama.
- Tell people you love them.
- Show appropriate affection.
- Spend quality time with loved ones.

- Telephone calls are a great way to express love much better than texting, although an "I love you" text is awesome to receive.
- Hire someone like me to teach you how to love yourself and others without fear.

Business

Love for our fellow human being need not cause angst. Merely caring about the well-being of your employees and co-workers demonstrates love of neighbor. We are all well aware that anything more is inappropriate. What is acceptable is sharing fun stories about your kids and family with co-workers. Talking about values, virtues like integrity, compassion and honesty is a roundabout way of telling people you are a loving person.

What you are striving for at work is "philia." C.S. Lewis talks about "philia" in his book The Four Loves. It is a general love for fellow humans and is the Greek word for brotherly love (think Philadelphia, the city of brotherly love). This is a benevolent, kindly love. The suggestions in the previous chapters all exemplify a loving caring work atmosphere. Here are a few other ways to encourage brotherly love at work:

- Acknowledge and congratulate individuals and teams on a job well done.
- Use company meetings to announce personal and company-wide successes.
- Start a mentor program for new hires with seasoned staff.
- Be sure to thank people every day for their efforts, positivity, anything of value they bring to the team.

- Stay positive.
- Encourage self-care and well-being with every person.
- Be authentic!
- Love your job and make it known.
- Hire someone like me to lead a series of "lunch and learns" or to advise your team on any or all topics in this book.

Conclusion

"You can take the Sicilian out of Sicily, but you can't take the Sicilian out of you."

Salvatore Taormina

As you can tell, I love my Sicilian heritage, the good, the bad and the ugly. I choose the beautiful, virtuous characteristics taught to me by my family, my Sicilian neighbors and my amazing friends in Sicily. Sicilians are the warmest, most loving, hospitable people I have ever met. I owe my Sicilian upbringing for the passion inside me to change the world, for loving each of you whether I know you personally or not.

I truly believe that the world can learn many lessons by melding the old school ways of Sicily with today's knowledge and technology. It is here where we live a purpose-driven life built on the foundation of love. Sicilians enjoy every day to the fullest by living the virtues of respect, loyalty, generosity, and work ethic combined with family, friends and a good-old meatball sandwich.

Family, food, wine and laughter, not always in that order, keep Sicilians bonded together. If you think about it, these hold true for every one of us. We merely have to let go of the resistance, fear and the wall around our hearts and start living and loving like the Sicilians. Can you imagine a world where we all lived a passionate purpose-driven life, loving without fear, like the Sicilians? I can, and I can teach you how. Dare to go back to the old country, old school values and old school relationships to move forward for a richer, more rewarding life. Know I love you all!

Acknowledgements

I cannot publish this book without thanking a few special people besides my beloved Grandma, to whom this book is dedicated.

Thank you and photo credits to Jersey Comedian Mike Marino who is on tour cracking everyone up all while "Making America Italian Again."

My editor, Ashli Richens, has been editing my books, advising me on publishing and putting up with my "Bostonese," bad language and my casual writing style for many years now. I am grateful to Ashli for her dedication to her craft, her advice and guidance. It was a relief to know Ashli would be editing my work, and I could offer not only my heart, but a book without grammatical errors.

My grammar school friend, Chris Ridgway, who took time out during the worst crisis of our lives to read this book and write a foreword for me. Chris and I came full circle as adults because we share a love for all things Sicilian. I am grateful for his friendship as well as his lovely wife Aubrey.

I have been working with Jamie Palmer, my business coach, since July 2018. Jamie believed in me when I did not believe in myself, constantly encouraged me and put up with me through countless major life adjustments. She not only coached me about my own business but taught me to trust myself and to own my gifts. I tip my hat to Jamie.

One other person in my life made this book possible, Francesco (Ciccio) Perna. Ciccio was my constant companion throughout my travels in Sicily. He drove me to the remote villages of Riesi and Pietraperzia where we found ourselves on a road that was actually a steep cobblestone staircase and deserted roads that were barely existent all while I was either screaming at the top of my lungs for my life or laughing until it hurt. Ciccio took me to nightclubs until almost dawn and kept me safe. He introduced me to his friends and made me his family. Ciccio took me to the grocery store where his brother-in-law is the butcher and helped me cook and clean to receive my new friends for dinner. He taught me the most about Sicilian life, language and food. He is still pissed that I do not eat seafood. Ciccio would consume anything from the sea, even if it were still swimming. I am forever grateful to my Scorta di Giorno e Scorta di Notte (escort by day and escort by night). I cannot wait for more adventures with him. Ciccio has a forever place in my heart. Grazie mille, Cich!

Here are a few more photos from Sicily:

Glossary

Casateddi: Sicilian half-moon shaped pockets of pastry with a sweet filling that may be either fried or baked. They can be considered a sweet version of a mini-calzone. Variations of these pastries are made all over southern Italy.

Cumpare (m): godfather, accomplice

Cummare (f): godmother, girlfriend

Paesano: fellow townsman, fellow villager

Paese: town, small town, rural center

Rispetto (Respect): a way of treating or thinking about something or someone. People respect others who are impressive for any reason, such as being in authority like a teacher or cop or being older like a grandparent. You show respect by being polite and kind.

Sfincione: a thick Sicilian pizza, or more precisely a focaccia, topped with tomatoes, onions, a few anchovies and perhaps grated *casciocavallo* cheese, seasoned with a dash of oregano. The Sicilian term "sfincia" alludes to sponges and the spongy, meaning that sfincione shares the same origin as sfinci.

Sfingi: larger pastry, filled with cannoli filling, typically ricotta cheese with powdered sugar.

Struffoli: Neapolitan dish made of deep fried balls of sweet dough. The dough is used in many Italian sweet treats such as *chiacchiere*. For struffoli, the dough is formed into balls about the size of marbles.

Zeppola (plural: Zeppole): A *zeppola* is an Italian pastry consisting of a deep-fried dough ball of varying size but typically about four inches in diameter. This fritter is usually topped with powdered sugar, filled with custard.

Grandma's Recipes

Cassateddi con Ricotta

4.5 cups flour

¾ cups granulated sugar

½ cup extra virgin olive oil

1 tablespoon of brandy

1 lemon

14 oz fresh ricotta

1.8 oz dark chocolate

1 egg white

cinnamon

powdered sugar

vegetable oil for frying

salt

- Mix the flour with half the sugar, 2 tablespoons of lemon juice, brandy, olive oil and a pinch of salt, incorporating the necessary water, until a firm dough.
- Cover it and let it rest for about 30 minutes.
- Sift the ricotta and pick it up in a bowl, stir in the remaining sugar, chocolate flakes and a pinch of cinnamon.

- Roll out the dough into a thin sheet and cut out of the disks, with a cutter or the edge of a glass.
- Distribute the above filling in small heaps; brush the edges with the beaten egg white with 1 teaspoon of water. Fold dough over filling and formed of ravioli.
- Fry *cassateddi* in hot oil; drain them on paper towels and serve hot, sprinkled with powdered sugar.

Ricotta Pie

Crust

1/2 stick butter

1/4 cup sugar

2 tbsp vanilla

4 egg yolks

pinch salt

2 cups flour

2 tsp baking powder

- Knead into a ball. If it is too, dry add small amounts of whole milk until you get a nice ball of dough.
- Divide into 2 balls.
- Stretch one into a greased cake pan on the bottom and sides.
- Leave the other dough for the top.

Filling

2 lbs dry ricotta (drain in cheesecloth if necessary)

1/2 cup sugar

4 egg whites

2 tsp vanilla

- Mix together gently.
- Pour into crust.
- Top with the second stretched dough.
- Apply an egg wash (beat 1 egg and paint the top of the pie using a pastry brush).

- Poke a couple of fork holes in the top crust to allow ventilation.
- Bake in a preheated 350° oven for 30-60 minutes. Using a toothpick, insert into pie. If it comes out clean, pie is done.

Dalla cucina di Nini D'Amico
From Nina D'Amico's Kitchen

Nina is a friend who was born in Terrasini, Sicily. She moved with her family to Gloucester, Massachusetts. Nina and her daughter, Maria Cracchiolo, continued the Sicilian bakery traditions in their Gloucester landmark: Caffe Sicilia. When you walk into Caffe Sicilia, it is as if you died and woke up in Terrasini. Nina shared this recipe with me:

Glazed Chocolate Balls

6 cups flour

1.5 cups sugar

1 cup chocolate cocoa

6 tsp. baking powder

1 cup Crisco

6 eggs, well beaten

1 Tbsp. vanilla

2 Tbsp. cloves

1 Tbsp. cinnamon

1 cup chocolate chips

1 cup chopped walnuts
(optional)

1 cup raisins (optional)

1 cup whole milk

Beat Crisco, sugar, eggs and vanilla until well blended. Add in all the dry ingredients. Include the optional ones, if desired. Hold the milk until last. Blend together. Now add the milk and blend. Form 2" balls and place 1" apart on a greased cookie sheet.

Bake in a 350° oven for about 10 minutes.

Make glaze by adding water one spoonful at a time to 1 cup confectioners' sugar until it is thick enough to drizzle and glaze the chocolate balls. Drizzle after they are removed from the oven. Let cool. Enjoy!

Frankie's Recipes

My dear friend and fellow Sicilian, Frankie Imbergamo, published his own cookbook. With permission from Frankie, I am sharing a couple here:

Frankie's Clams Casino

1.5 doz. fresh, live cherrystones, shucked (reserve clam shells in halves)

1 c. grated Romano Cheese

1 qt. minced clams

1.5 c. plain bread crumbs

1 stick of butter, melted

1/2 c. olive oil

1 Tbsp. fresh parsley, chopped

Pinch of Salt

Pinch of ground black pepper

Oil to drizzle

Lemon wedges

Tabasco sauce

In a bowl, add freshly shucked cherrystone meat, Romano cheese, minced clams, bread crumbs, melted butter, olive oil, parsley, garlic, salt and pepper. Mix together. Place mixture into clam shell halves. Drizzle with olive oil and bake at 350° for 10 minutes. Serve with lemon wedges and Tabasco sauce.

Frankie's Italian Meatloaf

2 lb. all-beef ground beef

1 c. plain breadcrumbs

1 large onion, chopped

4 eggs

1 (8 oz.) can tomato sauce

1 garlic clove chopped

1/4 c. grated Romano cheese

Salt

Pepper

In a large bowl, mix ground beef, bread crumbs, onion, eggs, 5 ounces tomato sauce (reserving rest for top of meatloaf), garlic, Romano cheese, salt, and pepper. Mix well. Place in a loaf pan. Spread reserved tomato sauce on top and sprinkle with salt and pepper. Cook 1 hour and 20 minutes, without covering, in a 350° oven.

Quotes

Other quotes from my fellow Sicilians upon being asked what was important to them in their Sicilian upbringing:

"My mom is half Sicilian half Abruzzese. Definitely the cultural aspect. Sicilians have a strong sense of culture and focus on respect and family. (As do all Italian cultures, but I've noticed the sense of respect stronger in southern cultures)"

Carla Balzano

"For me it was the respect to my family and elders."

Frank P Sgro

"Family and hard work ethic."

Lisa Travaglini

"My faith, respect for elders, stories, basement kitchen; cooking and eating well and being close knit family."

Lorraine Yezzi Kroell

"I think most who grew up in an Italian family, had respect, family first and Sunday macaroni dinner at Grandma's."

Mary Castaldo Blanchard

"My life has been positively impacted through our Italian traditions along with compassion and respect for one another. My dad's family was Sicilian & Mom's was from Northern Italy."

Debra Bertolino Owirka

About the Author

Steph Palermo was born into a Sicilian-American family just outside Boston, Massachusetts. All around, life was going to be a bit more difficult for her. Her home was equally filled with laughter and tears. Steph witnessed abuse, a gambling addiction and violence. At a very young age, Steph began to use food to find her "happy place."

Fast forward from the 1970s to 1999: four kids, a less-than-understanding husband, and an unhappy Steph catapulted onto the therapist's couch, where the dormant volcano spewed thirty years of repressed heartache on the lap of her shrink after years of trying to make her marriage work despite being unhappy.

Steph was finally able to walk away from her relationship and start on her path to creating a life where she could be happy again. She had an "aha" moment where she realized that we all have free will to choose happiness for ourselves. It was time to rebuild her life to be as happy as she could possibly be.

She began to subscribe to the DPP formula: desire, pursuit, and perseverance. Deep down, Steph had the desire to impact the lives of others and help them have the same revelation that she did about choosing happiness. She started living, having fun, dating, handling her own finances and working.

By creating her own business, Steph was able to discover her "why" in life. Helping others to create the life that they want and align with their true purpose is her passion, and this brings her the joy that she wants to share with others.

Steph Palermo is an intuitive Coach, influencer, talk show host, international speaker and published author. Steph draws from her life gifts of empathy and healing experiences, personality and sense of humor to share her message. Her Sicilian heritage and Boston wit make for an always uplifting and honest message. She realizes that everyone has two lives, and the second one begins when you acknowledge you only have one.

As a highly sensitive empath and entrepreneur, Steph combines her ability to feel the feelings of others and uses her motivational speaking skills to help others go from feeling grumpy to groovy every day. Her gift of being able to tap into other's emotional states helps her to create an honest and open relationship with her clients so that she can put them on the right path to improving their life. She believes that by aligning with your true purpose, recognizing your amazingness and changing your choices, you can alter your entire world. Steph is available for 1:1 coaching, speaking engagements, "lunch and learns" and workshops. Join Steph on one of her Feel Groovy healing retreats in Sicily where you will learn and experience firsthand how to live like a Sicilian.

Connect with Steph

Email: steph@juststeph.com
Website: www.juststeph.com
Facebook: https://www.facebook.com/juststeph1/
Twitter: https://twitter.com/stephpalermo
Linked In: https://www.linkedin.com/in/juststeph/
YouTube: https://www.youtube.com/channel/
UCK-PwnrCd1SzR3ScpFsYm2A?view_as=subscriber
Instagram: https://www.instagram.com/juststeph1/
iTunes: https://itunes.apple.com/us/podcast/
the-just-steph-show/id1120288646?mt=2
Soundcloud: https://soundcloud.com/steph-palermo

Members Only

Join Steph's exclusive community today! If you know you should be further along in life, or, have been struggling with unhealthy relationships, feeling unsatisfied and you are ready to level up your game, this is the place for you. Steph will personally guide you from where you are to a deeper understanding of who you are. Learn more about the topics in this book and Steph's other written works. This community is your go-to for support, encouragement and personal advancement. Get more of Just Steph and so many surprises and perks along the way. Come back with Steph to go forward. And remember this is for Members Only.

*FYI: A select number of VIP memberships are being offered.

Find out more here: https://juststeph.com/members-only/

Healing Retreat in Sicily: Reset Your Life

Let Steph show you first hand how to incorporate the Sicilian ways into your life by joining her on retreat in Sicily. Experience first-hand the sacred sites, food, wine and siesta together with discussions, intuitive coaching and healing with Steph. You will immerse in Sicilian culture and life. Her Sicilian friends are waiting for you! https://juststeph.com/feel-groovy-retreats-2/